HEALING COURAGE

MESSAGES OF LOVE, HOPE, AND STRENGTH

ALEXANDRA VILLARD DE BORCHGRAVE

Washington, DC

First published in the United States of America in 2014 by the

Light of Healing Hope Foundation
2801 New Mexico Avenue, N.W. #1224
Washington, DC 20007
www.lightofhealinghope.org

Art Direction and Design: Alexandra Villard de Borchgrave
Design: Henrique Siblesz, enlinea design
Photography: Neil Greentree, Freer Gallery of Art and the
Arthur M. Sackler Gallery

Printed and bound in the United States by Quality Graphics Printing Inc.
30% PCW

10 9 8 7 6 5 4 3 2 1

Library of Congress Cataloging-in-Publication Data

De Borchgrave, Alexandra Villard.
Healing Courage: Messages of Love, Hope, and Strength
Alexandra Villard de Borchgrave;
—1st ed.
ISBN-13: 978-0-9914418-0-8
ISBN-10: 099144180X

DEDICATION

For all those who have suffered
the adversity of life:

Though the wounds of life may
haunt the spirit,
Unspeakable sorrow leaving
ghosts of pain;
Abiding faith in
the goodness of man,
Allows love to transcend
this earthly plain.

Alexandra Villard de Borchgrave

CONTENTS

HEALING LIGHT

GARDEN OF LIGHT
BALANCE OF LIFE
COURAGE
INFINITE POSSIBILITIES
RISE WITH GRACE
NEW RESOLVE
TRANQUILITY

✳

HEAVENLY ORDER

HEAVENLY ORDER
CHILDREN OF PAIN
SPIRIT OF VALOR
A SEA OF TRANQUILITY
BEYOND EARTH'S RIM
SEARCHING
LIGHT OF GRACE

✳

BELOVED SPIRIT

JOURNEY
PATH
VALOR
LOVE
HARMONY
PEACE
SPIRIT

APPRECIATION

Alexandra Villard de Borchgrave's response to the events of 9/11 was to turn to poetry as both catharsis and communication. Determined to spread a message of hope in a bleak world, she formalized that communication in her first book, and less than a decade later, she produced three books. In each she has made her own journey in words, but she was equally determined to find a visual complement. In moving from her first book to her third, she has abandoned narrative for spirit. Yet the images form a sequence that has an over-arching narrative, as they follow the light and shades of a passing day, reminding us that, like all creatures, we are in this world for a fleeting moment.

Julian Raby, Dame Jillian Sackler Director
Arthur M. Sackler Gallery and the Freer Gallery of Art

Alexandra Villard de Borchgrave has creatively nested her voice within a variety of images, Mughal designs of India, Japanese painting and calligraphy, and Persian manuscript illustrations from Jami's *Haft awrang*. With meticulous attention to the subtleties of line and color, she studied each manuscript folio and selected elements that best captured and conveyed the spirit of her verses. Each page of *Beloved Spirit* sensitively juxtaposes a detail, whether a light soaked cloud, a tender sprig, or a lush blossoming flower, with a poem, subtly alternating rhythms of word and image and creating a harmonious whole.

Massumeh Farhad, Chief Curator and Curator of Islamic Art
Arthur M. Sackler Gallery and the Freer Gallery of Art

INTRODUCTION

Healing Courage: Messages of Love, Hope, and Strength is a compilation of poems from *Healing Light, Heavenly Order,* and *Beloved Spirit* and represents a decade of striving to bring comfort to those who are suffering.

In three endeavors to connect heartfelt reflections with beautiful images of the past, I have come to believe in an intimate moment of surrender, a time when the soul may connect with a higher being, light, spirit, or God, a part of which I am convinced resides within all of us. I believe this instance of release allows us to be open to creativity, take a step forward into the unknown, make untold mistakes along the way, and learn from them. It allows us to be vulnerable to sorrow, accepting of criticism and fosters a willingness to do better. It provides untapped courage in the face of terror and ultimately the peace with which to depart this life.

At this time of wearying world unrest and fragility, I am deeply grateful to have been given the opportunity to draw on the beauty expressed in these images of the past. To me, this beauty reveals a way to find order in chaos and leads us in turn to an expression of universal clarity, compassion, love, and healing.

In the exquisite words of the great Sufi poet Rumi,

> *"Rise up! The painter of Eternity has set to work one more time.*
> *To trace miraculous figures on this crazy curtain of the world.*
> *God has lit a fire to burn the heart of the universe…"*

 Alexandra Villard de Borchgrave
President and CEO, Light of Healing Hope Foundation

HEALING LIGHT

Let us see the beauty

within our souls

And succumb to a nurturing

that restores and consoles.

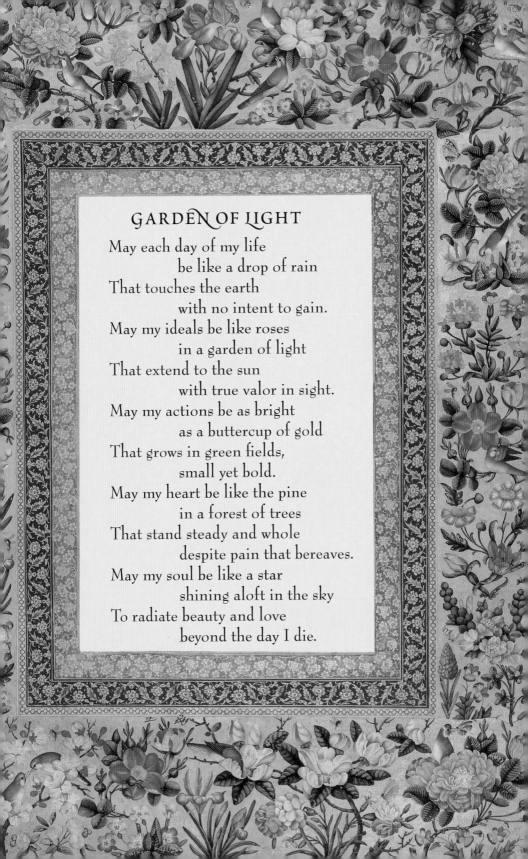

GARDEN OF LIGHT

May each day of my life
        be like a drop of rain
That touches the earth
        with no intent to gain.
May my ideals be like roses
        in a garden of light
That extend to the sun
        with true valor in sight.
May my actions be as bright
        as a buttercup of gold
That grows in green fields,
        small yet bold.
May my heart be like the pine
        in a forest of trees
That stand steady and whole
        despite pain that bereaves.
May my soul be like a star
        shining aloft in the sky
To radiate beauty and love
        beyond the day I die.

BALANCE OF LIFE

Still my heart
      in its desire for flight
And make clear
      how best my emotions to fight.
Scatter my fears
      like petals in the heat
To warm the earth
      beneath my trembling feet.
Prove the resilience
      of the stem as it bends
With patience and resolve
      in a wind that rends.
Reveal the harmony
      between the rose and the bee
As I seek the balance of life
      on both land and sea.
Crystallize my existence
      in a drop of dew
Sparkling, ephemeral
      with strivings of every hue.
Ignite my soul
      with the kiss of the sun
And spur good deeds
      until my time has come.

COURAGE

O Lord, color our souls
        with courage and strength
As we seek Your flame
        in the sun's evening length.
Free our hearts
        from anguish and woe
As we cast seeds of friendship
        to our most dangerous foe.
Conjure the will
        from spirits past
To ride by our side
        and hold us fast.
Overlook the flaws
        that lurk within
So we may find true greatness
        as a place to begin.
Grant us the joy
        of birds in flight
That we may reach unity and love
        at a greater height.

INFINITE POSSIBILITIES

Stretch my eyes beyond
        the horizon's blue line
To infinite possibilities
        only my soul can define.
Pour Thy love like water,
        clear and pure,
Into a heart now eager
        to achieve and endure.
Release my spirit
        like foam on a wave
To rise and swirl,
        seeking a path to pave.
Awaken new ideas for peace
        in all lands,
As I reach across the ocean
        to sundrenched sands.
Carry my wish for union
        with the surging tide
To the most distant corners
        where falcons ride.
Hearten my efforts
        to build bridges of gratitude,
Bringing all creeds together
        with boundless latitude.

RISE WITH GRACE

O Lord, set the stars to be
        my companions tonight
And fill my empty heart
        with their lustrous light.
Cast their shimmering dust
        upon my face
To halt the tears
        that run apace.
My longing is great
        for a love beyond measure
As I strive to discover
        life's inner treasure.
The fire within me
        has fallen low
And I need the warmth
        only You can bestow.
Guide my spirit
        to an inner source
Where courage and faith
        may reset my course.
Open my soul
        to Your radiant power
So that I may rise with grace
        in this hour.

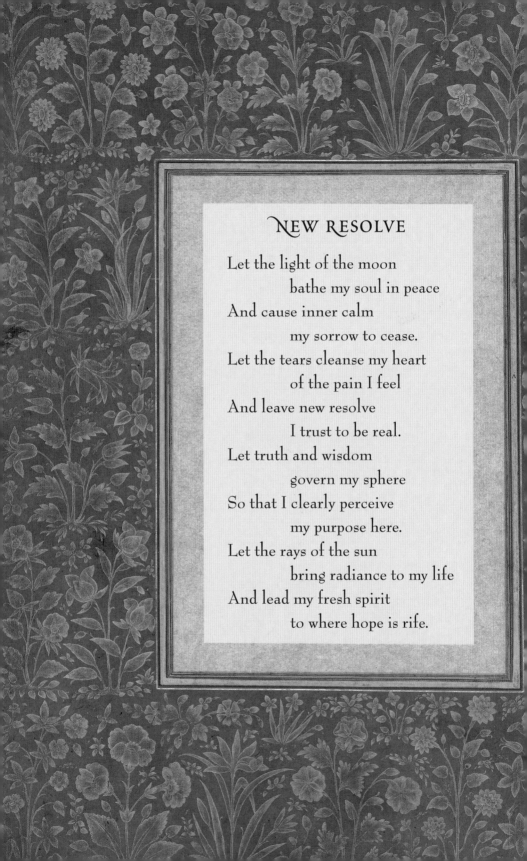

NEW RESOLVE

Let the light of the moon
   bathe my soul in peace
And cause inner calm
   my sorrow to cease.
Let the tears cleanse my heart
   of the pain I feel
And leave new resolve
   I trust to be real.
Let truth and wisdom
   govern my sphere
So that I clearly perceive
   my purpose here.
Let the rays of the sun
   bring radiance to my life
And lead my fresh spirit
   to where hope is rife.

TRANQUILITY

Bind the fragments of my heart
   with hope and peace
As the butterfly soothes the petal
   of a flower soon to cease.
Draw forth the strength
   beneath woe's dark shade
As moonlight breaks through the trees
   of a verdant, secret glade.
Urge me not to yearn
   for that which I cannot have
And instead trust in Your wisdom
   to provide a gentle salve.
Show me Your love
   in a young deer's sable eyes
As I enter the grassy lair
   where tranquility lies.

HEAVENLY ORDER

In the deepest crevasse

of the human soul

The kindness of heart

still thrives.

HEAVENLY ORDER

Like a leaf floating
    upward in the wind,
The soul begins
    its search,
To find through
    heavenly order
The beauty of
    this earth.

The spirit pursues its
    passionate goal
With each flow of
    life's breath,
To reach the
    absolute beauty
That conquers
    even death.

The mind that beholds
    all beauties of time
Within its
    inner eye,
Achieves an
    immortality
Heaven would
    not deny.

CHILDREN OF PAIN

Where goes this
    icy dagger
But deep within
    my heart,
To cut and tear with
    cruel intent
And break my
    soul apart?

Where can I find
    a refuge
From relentless
    searing pain,
When all about are
    shreds of truth
I struggle with
    in vain?

Where are the drops
    of wisdom
To cool my
    burning tears?
Perhaps I will only
    find them
Through a search of
    many years.

SPIRIT OF VALOR

The spirit that lies
 in every heart
Ascends
 with a radiant light,
And the human will
 to love and aspire
Brings the promise
 to achieve and excite.

Like a shooting star
 in a fading sky,
Courage
 within can prevail,
Leading us
 from a path of hate
To a peace,
 however frail.

While the breaking dawn
 may not reveal
The heavenly sight
 we seek;
It may, in its glory,
 herald the rise of
True valor in
 all its mystique.

A SEA OF TRANQUILITY

A sea of tranquility
    lies deep and still
In the core
    of the human soul;
Where the soundless depth
    of the treasure of life
Is found in
    small fragments made whole.

The search for harmony
    through a tide of faith
Leads the heart over
    waves of flaws;
To see humility in
    a grain of sand
Resides at
    the crux of the cause.

The purity of love carries
    crests of light
To create peace for
    all mankind;
For in the hidden shoals
    of wisdom and strength
Dwell the keys to
    hearts that are kind.

BEYOND EARTH'S RIM

Each step across a blade of grass
　　brings learning in its wake,
With fresh desire for greater strength
　　to win a higher stake.

The path must flow with bold attempts
　　to stretch beyond earth's rim,
And reach the edge of heaven's gate
　　with patience for a hymn.

Resilience now may lead the soul
　　to grow with inner grace,
Drawing genius from its depth
　　to burst with ardent pace.

The vines that hang with wondrous blooms
　　reflect that perfect state,
Where beauty in its rarest form
　　is free to meet its fate.

SEARCHING

Whatever the road
    one takes in life,
Let it lead past
    the selfish mind;
While tears may fall
    like leaves on a pond,
May stems of great
    longing unwind.

Though each step may
    try the bravest heart,
True purpose now
    wakens the need
To reach the shore
    of enlightened sight
With the strength to build
    a new creed.

The secret world of
    the searching heart
Is opened by
    a loving glance,
Allowing hidden dreams
    of the soul
To spire into
    limitless chance.

LIGHT OF GRACE

The joy of love is in the stars that
    cloak the earth at night,
And hold the woe of sins at length
    till early morning sight.

The sun reveals the blooms of hope
    that grow with fine intent,
Taking the pain of loss inside
    with pride and faith unbent.

A thousand leaves of hallowed truths
    surround the heart with vines,
To protect the soul from savage deeds
    through fiery battle lines.

The spirit of the world endures
    in heaven's warm embrace,
Defying flames of cruel distress
    to reach the light of grace.

BELOVED SPIRIT

Love before the

break of day has begun;

Love with a heart

reaching many or one.

JOURNEY

The Journey begins with
    the paling moon,
Heavenly stars bidding
    their soft farewell;
The cool fresh earth before
    the day's first ray,
Reveals the sacred site where
    hope may dwell.

The stream of life carries
        the soul's desire,
Clear waves of truth lapping at
        steps of sand;
The tender light of
        the horizon's new dawn,
Draws the yearning heart to
        a distant land.

Though the wounds of life may
        haunt the spirit,
Unspeakable sorrow leaving
        ghosts of pain;
Abiding faith in
        the goodness of man,
Allows love to transcend
        this earthly plain.

PATH

Wake to the shadows
of the night's last breath
as graces of light lift
their misty veil;
Gather up the silent
tendrils of dreams
to fashion the path
where love will prevail.

Though golden vines of passion
may entwine,
perfumed hyacinth cajole
and entreat,
Remain true to the rose's
pure white soul
with its scent of faith,
fragrant but discreet.

While sharp stinging nettles
of distress abound,
taunting the weary heart
once and again;
Live on as the rose's stem
— unbroken,
alive with courage and
honor to gain.

VALOR

Give of the heart when
the world is breaking,
See new horizons though
sight is fading.
Love with the secret
currents of passion,
Connect with strands of
sorrow's compassion.
Though lies and despair may
pervade the air,
Weeping rains pour into
rivers of grief,
Human valor may flow up
from the deep
To bring all in need
to angels' kind keep.

LOVE

Treasure a love that burns so fine

It defies the rule and passage of time;

Deeper than the sea, softer than a song,

Desire sees no fault in rapture sublime.

Like a single white star emerging at night
In the vastness of an immortal joy,
The dream will survive in eternal love,
No human error or death may destroy.

Pure silken threads lace the heavens' line
In homage to the dying crimson sun;
And the light carries the heart beyond all grief
To a love, undenied, two souls as one.

HARMONY

There is such a point
of infinite light
Where the sun and the moon
wed in times of old,
And the night and the day
become as one —
A chalice of joy
too dazzling to hold.

With glittering stardust
on silver clouds,
Radiant harmony
surrounds the soul,
And a life too fragile for
earth's harsh mold,
Is inscribed on Heaven's
most cherished scroll.

In a timeless place of
no hour or land,
Where the soul is free
to seek soaring dreams,
The heart will know the
true secret of life —
To steer love to others
by gracious means.

PEACE

A moment may come at the rarest time,
　　When the moon turns to gold and stars to pearls,
And the soul in need gains a precious sphere
　　Of healing peace free of perilous swirls.

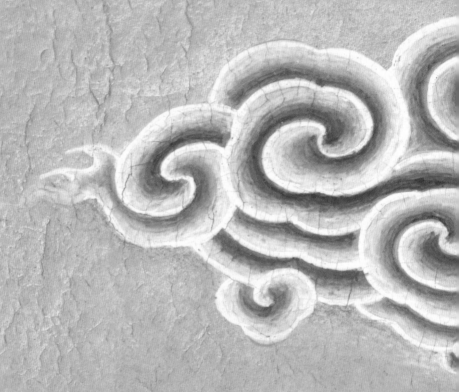

On this half way path to angelic heights,
　　When the light and dark dissolve into mist,
Hatred and jealousy are cast aside
　　And shades of love find reason to exist.

Carry onward the gentle standard of worth,
    Love first all others beyond self or land;
Then brightness will surely fill this sad world,
    Bringing forth new greatness as once was planned.

SPIRIT

On a night when the course
of life is run,
And the heart and the light
at last entwine,
The beauty of all the world
now unfolds
In breathless grace only
faith may define.

In this instant's bliss,
when innocence thrives,
And stars hang so low as
to touch the heart,
The soul may arise to
reach the divine,
Leaving imprints on earth
as works of art.

At the hour when planets
halt in their path,
To receive the noble and sinner
as one;
The truth of a fortune,
dismal or fine,
Matters not when Heaven's
kindness is won.

This collection would not have been possible without the exceptional courtesy of the Freer Gallery of Art and the Arthur M. Sackler Gallery of Art, and we would like to extend our deepest thanks to Julian Raby, The Dame Jillian Sackler Director of the Arthur M. Sackler Gallery and the Freer Gallery of Art, and the entire staff for their generous and invaluable assistance. We would also like to thank the Trustees of the British Museum; the National Gallery of Victoria, Melbourne, Australia; and the Harvard Art Museums/Arthur M. Sackler Museum.

ARTWORK
FROM
HEALING LIGHT

GARDEN OF LIGHT   Freer Gallery of Art, Smithsonian Institution, Washington, DC DETAIL: Jahangir entertains Shah Abbas. Page from the St.Petersburg Album. (South Asian, Mughal, ca. 1620. Purchase, F1942.16a) BORDER: Allegorical representation of Emperor Jahangir and Shah Abbas of Persia. Page from the St.Petersburg Album. Abu'l Hasan. (South Asian, Mughal, ca. 1618. Purchase, F1945.9a)

BALANCE OF LIFE   DETAIL & BORDER: A poem by Amir Shahi. Page from the late Shah Jahan Album. Mir-Ali Sultani. (South Asian, Mughal, 16th Century. Arthur M. Sackler Gallery, Smithsonian Institution, Washington, DC. Purchase, Smithsonian Unrestricted Funds, Smithsonian Collections Acquisition Program and Dr. Arthur M. Sackler, S1986.90)

COURAGE   DETAIL: Maharana Sangram Singh Hunting Crane at Nahar Magra. (Udaipur, Rajasthan, India ca. 1720. National Gallery of Victoria, Melbourne, Australia. Felton Bequest, 1980) BORDER: Equestrian Portrait of Shah Jahan. (South Asian, Rajput, ca.1750–1770. Arthur M. Sackler Gallery, Smithsonian Institution, Washington, DC. Purchase, Smithsonian Unrestricted Funds, Smithsonian Collections Acquisition Program and Dr. Arthur M. Sackler, S1986.415)

ARTWORK
FROM
HEALING LIGHT
CONTINUED

INFINITE POSSIBILITIES — DETAIL: Krishna and Radha in Procession to a Palace Sunset. (Rajasthan, Nathadwara, ca. 1900. © The Trustees of the British Museum) BORDER: Calligraphy. Mir Imad al-Husayni. Page from the St.Petersburg Album. Borders: Muhammad-Baqir and Muhammad-Hadi. (South Asian, Mughal, ca. 1660. Freer Gallery of Art, Smithsonian Institution, Washington, DC. Purchase, F1996.1b)

RISE WITH GRACE — Freer Gallery of Art, Smithsonian Institution, Washington, DC DETAIL: Rama, Lakshmana, Vishmavitra. From a Persian translation of the Ramayana. Ghulam 'Ali. (South Asian, Mugal, late 16th century. Gift of Charles Lang Freer, F1907.271.34) BORDER: Calligraphy. Page from the St.Petersburg Album. Imad al-Hasani. (South Asian, Mughal, ca. 1608. Purchase, F1942.16b)

NEW RESOLVE — Freer Gallery of Art, Smithsonian Institution, Washington, DC DETAIL: The Gopies Search for Krishna from a Bhagavata Purana. Guler-Kangra. (South Asian, Pahari, ca. 1780. Purchase, F1930.84) BORDER: Portrait of Abd ar-Rahim, Khan Khanan. Hashim. (South Asian, Mughal, ca. 1626. Purchase, F1939.50a)

TRANQUILITY — DETAIL: Bhimsen, Krishna Hunting by Moonlight (ca.1781. Harvard Art Museums/Arthur M. Sackler Museum, Gift of Stuart Cary Welch, Jr. in memory of Jacqueline Bouvier Kennedy Onassis, 1995.102 Photo: Imaging Department © President and Fellows of Harvard College) BORDER: Calligraphy. Page from the St.Petersburg Album. (South Asian, Mughal, ca. 17th century. Freer Gallery of Art, Smithsonian Institution, Washington, DC. Purchase, F1942.18b)

ARTWORK
FROM
HEAVENLY ORDER

Artworks are courtesy of the
Freer Gallery of Art,
Smithsonian Institution, Washington, DC
Gift of Charles Lang Freer

HEAVENLY ORDER
Utaibon, 18–19th centuries,
from the Rare Book Collection, Freer
Gallery of Art, Arthur M. Sackler Gallery,
Smithsonian Institution Libraries
822–U8–Utaibon20

CHILDREN OF PAIN
Imperial Anthology, Kokinshu
Hon'ami Koetsu, 1558–1637
Tawaraya Sotatsu, fl. ca. 1600–1643
Japan, Momoyama or Edo period,
early 17th century
F1903.309 sec 11 det 1

SPIRIT OF VALOR
Mimosa tree, poppies, hollyhocks, and
other flowers. Sosetsu, active mid–17th
century. Japanese, Edo period, 1630–1670
F1902.92 det 2.2

A SEA OF TRANQUILITY
Summer and autumn flowers
Japanese, Edo period, 1615–1868
F1896.82 det 2

BEYOND EARTH'S RIM
Summer and autumn flowers
Japanese, Edo period, 1615–1868
F1896.82 det 4.2

SEARCHING
Mimosa tree, poppies, hollyhocks,
and other flowers
Sosetsu, active mid–17th century
Japanese, Edo period, 1630–1670
F1902.92 det 1.2

LIGHT OF GRACE
Mimosa tree, poppies, hollyhocks, and
other flowers. Sosetsu, active mid–17th
century. Japanese, Edo period, 1630–1670
F1902.92 det 1

ARTWORK
FROM
BELOVED SPIRIT

ON THE DVD: Music Videos with animated artwork, poem readings, and classical music.

GARDEN OF LIGHT   Air From Suite No 3 in D Major, BWV 1068
(2:52)   Johann Sebastian Bach
Karl Richter & Munchener Bach Orchester
Universal Music Group

BALANCE OF LIFE   Panis Angelicus, Cesar Franck
(3:10)   Julian Lloyd Webber & Stokowski/Philadephia
Orchestra, Universal Music Group

RISE WITH GRACE   Oboe Concerto in D Minor: II
(2:58)   Alessandro Marcello
Paul Angerer & Southwest German Chamber
Orchestra, Helmut Hucke, Oboe
Warner/Chappell Production Music

A SEA OF TRANQUILITY   Symphony No 5 in C Sharp Minor: IV
(2:46)   Gustav Mahler, London Symphony Orchestra
& Harold Faberman Poem
Warner/Chappell Production Music

SEARCHING   Adagio For Strings, Op.11
(2:33)   Samuel Barber, Sir Neville Mariner &
Academy of St.Martin of the Fields Orchestra
Universal Music Group. Musical Composition
© G.Shermer, Inc.

LIGHT OF GRACE   L'Arlésienne Suite #1: III
(2:45)   Georges Bizet, Myung-Whun Chung
& Orchestre de L'Opéra Bastille,
Universal Music Group

LOVE   Xerxes: Ombra Mai Fu: Largo
(3:07)   George Frideric Handel
Apollo Symphony Orchestra
Music Loops.Com

HARMONY   Orpheus and Eurydice
(2:34)   'Dance of the Blessed Spirits'
Christoph Willibald Gluck, Andras Korodi
& Budapest Philharmonic Orchestra
Warner/Chappell Production Music

SPIRIT   Motet in D Major for Choir and Orchestra
(2:35)   K. 618: Ave Verum Corpus
Wolgang Amadeus Mozart
Warner/Chappell Production Music

TOTAL (25:19)

LIGHT
OF
HEALING HOPE®
FOUNDATION

The Light of Healing Hope Foundation is a 501 (c)(3) charitable organization dedicated to providing books of hope as gifts to hospitals to comfort patients and their families at a time of adversity. We provide gift packages that include a book of hope, a music video DVD, and a Healing Notes booklet in which patients may write messages to encourage the healing process. We are committed to bringing comfort to all those who are suffering by offering pathways to spiritual hope, peace, and healing. We have given our gift packages to hospitals and hospices nationwide including Walter Reed National Military Medical Center, Fisher House, Wounded Warrior Project, NIH, Johns Hopkins Hospital, and INOVA Hospitals.

www.LightOfHealingHope.org

Striving to bring comfort to those who are suffering.

"Thank you for bettering the lives of patients
and families during the fight of their lives."
~**Amanda Myers**, Guest Services Coordinator,
Hackerman-Patz Pavilion at Johns Hopkins

"The book helps keep my mind in a better place
and remain positive and hopeful."
~**ProMedica Patient**, The Hickman Cancer Center at
the Flower Hospital, Ohio

"Alexandra Villard de Borchgrave's poems
fill a patient's inner void with hope, which contributes
significantly to the overall healing process in cancer."
~**Dr. David Sidransky**, Oncology,
Johns Hopkins Medical School

"My family and I would like to thank you for the wonderful
book. It will be read many times over, as we all deal with
the loss of a wonderful, brave young man, son, and brother
(12.23.06). God Bless you from a Soldier's Family."

Alexandra Villard de Borchgrave has built a reputation as a photojournalist, author, and poet over the past forty years. Her photographs have appeared on the covers of internationally renowned publications, such as *Newsweek* and *Paris Match*. She is the co-author of *Villard: The Life and Times of an American Titan* (Nan A. Talese/Doubleday), a biography of her great grandfather, railroad magnate and financier Henry Villard, who masterminded the creation of General Electric. Alexandra Villard de Borchgrave is also the author of *Healing Light: Thirty Messages of Love, Hope, and Courage; Heavenly Order: Twenty Five Meditations of Wisdom and Harmony;* and *Beloved Spirit: Pathways to Love, Grace, and Mercy* (Glitterati Incorporated). Mrs. de Borchgrave founded the Light of Healing Hope Foundation, a 501(c)(3) non-profit organization, in 2010 in the hope of bringing comfort and healing to those in need.